MAKE-IT MOD

MAKE AN
AMUSEMENT
PARK

Anna Claybourne

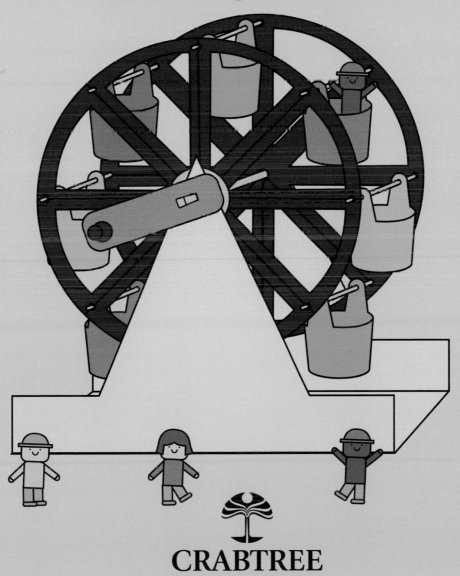

CRABTREE
PUBLISHING COMPANY
WWW.CRABTREEBOOKS.COM

CRABTREE
PUBLISHING COMPANY
WWW.CRABTREEBOOKS.COM

Published in Canada
Crabtree Publishing
616 Welland Avenue
St. Catharines, ON
L2M 5V6

Published in the United States
Crabtree Publishing
PMB 59051
350 Fifth Ave, 59th Floor
New York, NY 10118

Published in 2020 by Crabtree Publishing Company

First published in Great Britain in 2019 by Wayland
Copyright © Hodder and Stoughton, 2019

Author: Anna Claybourne

Editorial director: Kathy Middleton

Editors: Elise Short, Elizabeth DiEmanuele

Proofreader: Wendy Scavuzzo

Design and illustration: Collaborate

Production coordinator and prepress: Ken Wright

Print coordinator: Katherine Berti

Printed in the U.S.A./122019/CG20191101

The website addresses (URLs) included in this book were valid at the time of going to press. However, it is possible that contents or addresses may have changed since the publication of this book. No responsibility for any such changes can be accepted by either the author or the Publisher.

Note: In preparation of this book, all due care has been exercised with regard to the instructions, activities, and techniques depicted. The publishers regret that they can accept no liability for any loss or injury sustained. Always get adult supervision and follow manufacturers' advice when using electric and battery-powered appliances.

Library and Archives Canada Cataloguing in Publication

Title: Make an amusement park / Anna Claybourne.
Other titles: Fairground
Names: Claybourne, Anna, author.
Description: Series statement: Make-it models |
 Previously published under title: Fairground.
 London: Wayland, 2019. | Includes index.
Identifiers: Canadiana (print) 20190200332 |
 Canadiana (ebook) 201902003340 |
 ISBN 9780778773535 (hardcover) |
 ISBN 9780778773597 (softcover) |
 ISBN 9781427124920 (HTML)
Subjects: LCSH: Amusement rides—Models—Juvenile literature.
 | LCSH: Amusement parks—Models—Juvenile literature. |
 LCSH: Models and modelmaking—Juvenile literature.
Classification: LCC GV1859 .C53 2020 |
 DDC j791.06/80228—dc23

Library of Congress Cataloging-in-Publication Data

Names: Claybourne, Anna, author.
Title: Make an amusement park / Anna Claybourne.
Description: New York, New York : Crabtree Publishing
 Company, 2020. | Series: Make-it models | Includes index.
Identifiers: LCCN 2019043486 (print) |
 LCCN 2019043487 (ebook) |
 ISBN 9780778773535 (hardcover) |
 ISBN 9780778773597 (paperback) |
 ISBN 9781427124920 (ebook)
Subjects: LCSH: Amusement parks--Design and construction--
 Juvenile literature.
Classification: LCC GV1851.A35 C57 2020 (print) |
 LCC GV1851.A35 (ebook) | DDC 791.06/8--dc23
LC record available at https://lccn.loc.gov/2019043486
LC ebook record available at https://lccn.loc.gov/2019043487

CONTENTS

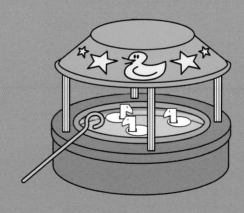

ALL THE FUN OF THE AMUSEMENT PARK!

Amusement parks and festivals have existed for many years, but when amusement parks first started, they only had stalls, shows, and contests. Amusement parks and rides became popular in the 1800s, after the invention of steam and electric power.

Since then, designers have come up with bigger, faster, and more exciting rides, such as thrilling **corkscrew roller coasters**, and super-sized **Ferris wheels**. You can find rides like these at amusement parks and festivals all over the world.

If you love amusement parks and rides, this book is for you. You'll find out how to design and build your own roller coaster, Ferris wheel, swing, **carousel**, and lots more.

MAKE IT YOUR OWN!

You can make the projects exactly as instructed, or make them your own! Use the instructions as a starting point, then make up your own designs.

Make a carousel with dragons instead of horses, a tall swing ride, or a double Ferris wheel. You can even invent your own ride! After all, today's ride designers create rides for a living. One day, that could be your job, too!

MAKE-IT MATERIALS

The projects in this book use items you can find at home, such as reusable containers, packaging, and basic arts and crafts equipment. If you don't have what you need, you can usually get it at a craft store, grocery store, or by ordering online. Go to page 31 for a list of useful sources.

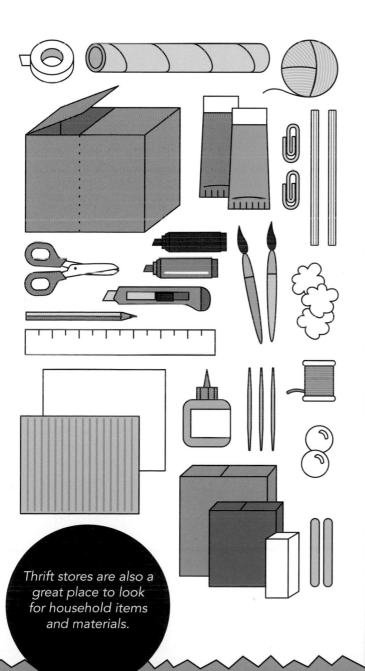

Thrift stores are also a great place to look for household items and materials.

SAFETY ALERT!

For some of the projects, you will need to use sharp tools such as a craft knife, wire clippers, or a bradawl (a tool for making holes). Or you might want to use an electric appliance such as a hot **glue gun**.

For anything involving sharp objects, heat, or electricity, always ask an adult to help and supervise. Make sure you keep items like these in a safe place.

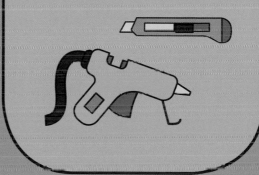

CAN I USE THIS?

Before getting started, make sure your containers and household items are clean and ready to use. Also check for permission to use them to make your rides. Buckle your seat belt, you're ready to begin!

HELTER-SKELTER

A **helter-skelter** is a traditional United Kingdom amusement park ride that is more than 100 years old!

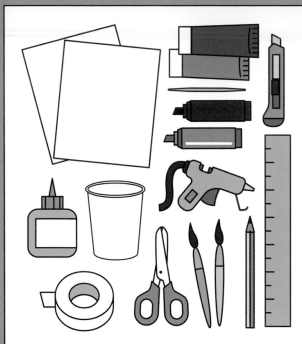

WHAT YOU NEED

- Two large sheets of smooth white card stock (8.5 x 11 inches (216 x 279 mm) or bigger)
- A paper cup
- Scissors or a craft knife
- Clear tape
- Superglue or a glue gun
- Paints and paintbrushes, or markers
- A ruler and a pencil
- A toothpick or a wooden skewer

For the large sheets of card stock, you could also use the backs of large pads of construction paper, or card stock from large packaging boxes, as long as it is smooth and flexible, not corrugated. (Corrugated is when the paper has ridges, like cardboard.).

 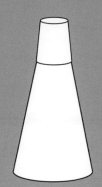

1 Curl one sheet of card stock into a cone shape, with a narrow top of about 2.5 inches (6 cm) across. Tape it together on the inside. Trim the ends so it can stand by itself.

2 Trim the rim off of the paper cup and check that it fits on top of the cone. If it doesn't fit, trim the top of the cone.

3 Draw a door and windows on the paper cup. Carefully cut them out. Glue the cup on top of the cone. Decorate the tower with markers or paints and let it dry.

4 On a sheet of card stock, use a ruler and pencil to draw a row of dots across the middle of the sheet. The dots should be around 1 inch (3 cm) apart. Starting in the middle, draw a spiral that passes through each of the dots. Keep drawing the spiral until you get to the edge of the card stock.

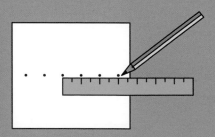 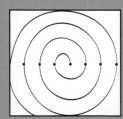

5 Carefully cut out the spiral and paint it. When the paint is dry, open it out and lower it over the tower.

6 Attach the spiral so that it wraps around the tower from the top (just below the door) to the bottom, just like a slide. Cut off any parts you don't need at the ends.

0.5 inches
(1 cm)

1 inch
(2.5 cm)

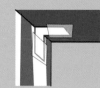

7 Cut small rectangles of card stock that are 0.5 inches (1 cm) wide and 1 inch (2.5 cm) long. Fold them in half. To hold the slide in place, glue or tape the rectangles underneath different parts of the spiral.

4 inches
(10 cm)

1 inch
(2.5 cm)

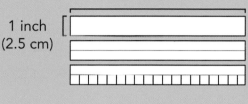

8 Cut strips of card stock that are 1 inch (2.5 cm) wide and 4 inches (10 cm) long. Fold them in half down the long side. On one side of the fold, cut slits about 0.5 inches (1 cm) apart. These slits will help you curve the paper to make a railing. Decorate them, then glue them along the edge of the slide.

9 Cut another door into the base of the tower. Make and decorate a paper flag. Glue your flag to the skewer or toothpick and stick it onto the top of the tower.

TIP
Traditional helter-skelters often have a red and white striped pattern, but you can use any color or pattern you like.

THE SCIENCE PART!
The helter-skelter uses **gravity** to pull the rider down to the bottom. The longer you slide, the faster you go!

SWING RIDE

The swing ride makes riders fly out sideways as they spin around. These rides can be any height. Some are close to the ground and others are high in the sky!

WHAT YOU NEED

- A shallow box, such as a box of chocolates with a lid
- Two cardboard tubes, one slightly narrower than the other
- A round cardboard box
- A pencil
- Scissors or a craft knife
- Clear tape
- Superglue or a glue gun
- White paper and card stock
- Paints and paintbrushes or markers
- White glue
- Small metal paper clips
- Thread
- A bradawl or a sewing needle
- A wooden craft stick

1 Take the wider cardboard tube and place it onto the middle of the shallow box lid. Trace the shape so you draw a circle. Set the paper towel tube aside. Then carefully cut a hole in the box lid that is slightly smaller than the circle you drew. This will create a tight fit for the next step.

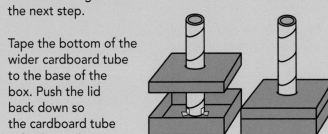

2 Tape the bottom of the wider cardboard tube to the base of the box. Push the lid back down so the cardboard tube is firmly in place.

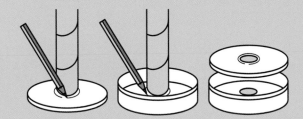

3 Use the narrower cardboard tube to trace a circle in the lid of the round cardboard box. (Similar to the previous steps, the circle should be in the middle.) Cut a hole in the lid that is slightly smaller than the circle you drew. Do the same with the base of the round box.

4 Push the narrower tube through both holes, leaving 1 inch (2.5 cm) sticking out at the top. Trim the ends of the empty cardboard tubes if needed so that the narrower one fits inside the wider one. You may also need to trim so that the round cardboard box can turn.

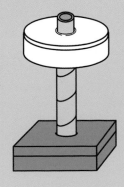

5 Decorate the ride. You can use paint mixed with white glue to make it stick. Or, you can use white paper to cover the ride and color in with markers.

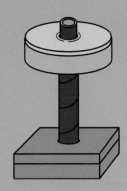

6 Bend a paper clip into a square. Cut a piece of card stock the same width as the square and four times as long. Cut one end of it into a narrow strip. Fold the card stock to make a seat that fits over the sides of the square. Glue it in place.

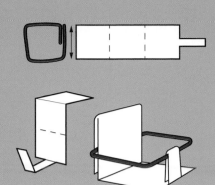

7 Loop a long piece of thread under the folded back of the chair. Cut two slits in the front of the chair. Loop another piece of thread through them.

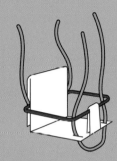

8 Take the lid off the round box and make holes around the edge of its base. Push the ends of the thread through a hole. Adjust them so that the chair hangs straight, then tape them in place. Add more chairs all around the edge, then put the lid back on.

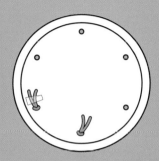

9 Using a craft knife or scissors, make a slit through the top of the narrow tube, above the round lid. Fit a craft stick through it, so that you can turn the ride.

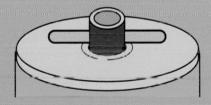

THE SCIENCE PART!

This ride works using **centrifugal force**. As an object is turned around in a circle, centrifugal force also makes it pull outward. This makes the chairs fly out sideways.

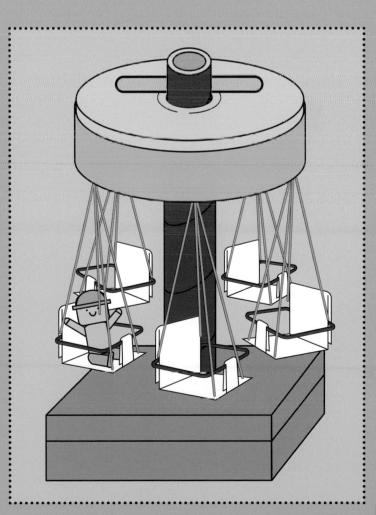

AMUSEMENT PARK GAMES

Any good amusement park has plenty of games, where you can test your skills and win a prize.

WHAT YOU NEED

- Small and medium-sized square cardboard boxes
- Medium-sized round (cardboard) box
- A round plastic lid at least 1 inch (2.5 cm) deep
- White paper and card stock
- Scissors or a craft knife
- Superglue or a glue gun
- Clear tape
- Paints and paintbrushes or markers
- White glue
- A bradawl or a sewing needle
- A pencil
- A paper bowl
- Four non-bendy straws
- Metal paper clips
- A sheet of craft foam
- A silver pen or marker
- Small round beads

FOR A CAN KNOCKDOWN GAME:

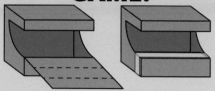

1 On a square box, draw the shape of the stall that will hold your carnival game. Cut out the sides. To make a counter, fold the cardboard at the front of the box twice, then tape it to the inside of the box.

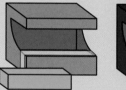

2 Make a counter at the back of the stall by using a smaller box, such as a toothpaste box. Decorate the stall with markers or paints mixed with white glue to make it stick. Leave it to dry.

3 Cut a sign shape out of card stock. Decorate the sign, then glue or tape it to the front of the stall. For the cans, roll paper strips into cylinders. Color them silver and decorate them if you like. Stack them in pyramids on the back counter.

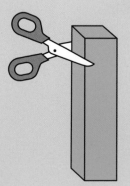

4 Cut the end off a small box to make a tray. Color it silver, too. Glue it to the front counter. Fill it with beads to use as balls for knocking down the cans.

FOR A HOOK-A-DUCK STALL:

1 Trace the round plastic lid onto the middle of the round box. Cut out a hole, just inside the line of the circle you drew. Glue the lid into the hole to make a shallow pool.

2 Use a bradawl or sewing needle to make four holes around the sides of the box. Use a pencil to make the holes bigger. Fit four straws into the holes. Tape or glue the straws in place inside the round box.

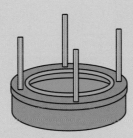

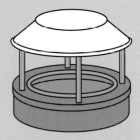

3 Trim the straws down to about 4 inches (10 cm). Glue an upside-down paper bowl on top as a roof. Add a cardboard sign if you like. Decorate the stall and leave it to dry.

4 Make ducks from craft foam. Cut out ovals for the bodies of the ducks. Cut out head and neck shapes with downward-pointing beaks for the remaining parts. To make the ducks from these shapes, make slits in the ovals and fit the necks into them.

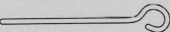

5 To make the hooks, straighten out metal paper clips and bend one end into a hook shape. Carefully pour water into the pool and float the ducks on it.

MAKE IT FUN!

• To add prizes, make hooks from paper clips and attach them to the stalls. Hang up tiny dolls, balls, or other toys.
• Can you design and make other types of stalls?

TIP

You can try these games yourself, even though they're model-sized! Try hooking a duck by its beak with the tiny hook, or put a bead on the front counter and flick it at the tin cans.

FERRIS WHEEL

A Ferris wheel is one of the most spectacular sights at the amusement park. Ferris wheels are also popular attractions outside amusement parks, with increasingly bigger wheels being built in city centers around the world.

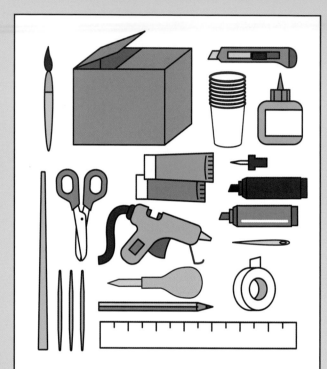

WHAT YOU NEED

- A large, strong **corrugated cardboard** box (at least 13.5 inches (35 cm) tall)
- A chopstick
- Wooden skewers
- A bradawl or a sewing needle
- Eight paper cups
- A tack
- Scissors or a craft knife
- Superglue or a glue gun
- Clear tape
- A ruler and a pencil
- Paints and paintbrushes or markers

1 On one side of the box, draw a line about 1.5 inches (4 cm) up from the base. Draw a large triangle in the middle about 12 inches (30 cm) tall and 8 inches (20 cm) wide at the base.

12 inches (30 cm)

1.5 inches (4 cm)

8 inches (20 cm)

2 Cut out the triangle, the 1.5-inch (4 cm) strip, and half of the base of the box, so that you have a piece that looks like this.

3 Do the same with the other side of the box, making two matching pieces. Trim each base piece to be about 2 inches (5 cm) wide. Stick them together using strong tape.

2 inches (5 cm)

4 Cut two circles of cardboard 1.5 inches (3 cm) wide. Glue them inside each of the triangle-shaped sides at the top. Use a bradawl or sewing needle to make holes through the middle of the circle and at the tip of the triangle.

1.5 inches (3 cm)

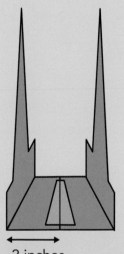

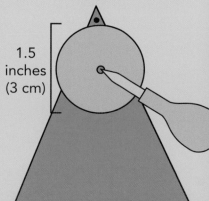

5 Use a pencil to make the holes bigger. Push the chopstick through the holes. Check that it can turn easily. You can now decorate the base with paint or markers.

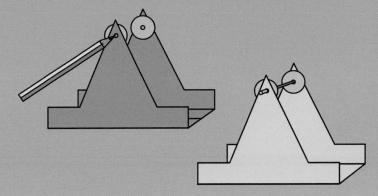

6 Take the two sides of the box that you haven't used yet. Draw a circle on each of them, about 12 inches (30 cm) wide. (Draw around an object that's roughly the right size, such as a large dinner plate.)

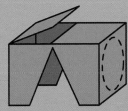

7 Cut out the circles. Draw a dot in the middle of each circle and use a ruler to draw a line across. Draw another line at a right angle, and two more lines between them to make eight pieces.

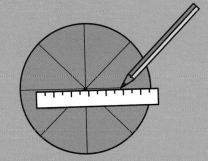

8 In one of the sections, draw a triangle 0.5 inches (1 cm) inside of the edges. Carefully cut it out. Use it as a **template** to draw and cut out triangles in the rest of the sections. Do this for both wheels.

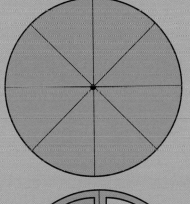
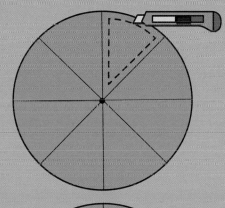
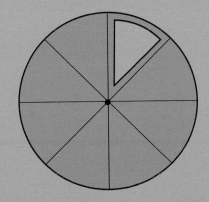

TURN THE PAGE TO CONTINUE ...

9 Use a bradawl or sewing needle to make a hole in the middle of each circle. Use a pencil to make it slightly larger (not much). If you like, decorate the wheels.

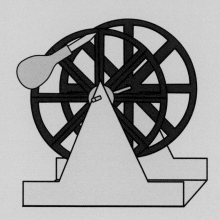

10 Place the two wheels inside the base piece. Push the chopstick through the holes in the base and through the two wheels. It should fit tightly on the wheels. Move the wheels apart so that they almost touch the sides of the base.

11 Check that you can turn the chopstick handle around to make the wheels turn. Line up the **spokes** in the two wheels. At the end of each spoke, make small holes through both wheels with the bradawl or sewing needle.

12 Now make the eight baskets. For each basket, draw a basket shape on a paper cup, with two arms pointing up at the sides. Cut out the basket shapes.

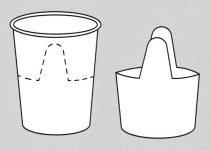

13 Poke holes through the tops of the arms. Make them larger by using a pencil (or hole punch). If you like, decorate the baskets.

14 Attach the basket to the wheel. First line up the holes of the wheel with the holes of the basket. Push the wooden skewer through so that the basket hangs. Trim off the ends if they stick out.

15 Repeat step 14 for all the baskets. Once all the baskets are in place, check that they are able to swing freely when you turn the wheel. If they don't, move the arm holes down.

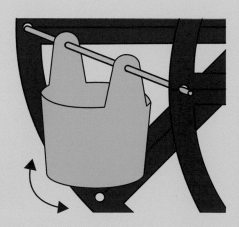

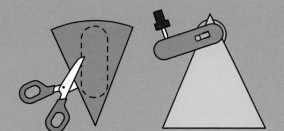

16 Cut a strip of cardboard that is a little more than 0.5 inches wide (2 cm) and 2 inches (5 cm) long. Cut a small square hole in one end. Fit it onto the chopstick handle. Stick a tack in the other end to make a turning handle.

TIP
Sit small toys in the baskets to ride the Ferris wheel!

TIP
You may need to adjust the position of the wheel, chopstick, or base slightly to make everything work.

THE SCIENCE PART!

The world's biggest Ferris wheels are more than 525 feet (160 m) tall! That's as high as a skyscraper with 50 floors. Instead of open baskets, these giant wheels often have covered pods or capsules. Some have as many as 60 pods!

TAKE IT FURTHER

Ferris wheels often have lights, making them look even more amazing when night falls. You could light up your Ferris wheel by attaching glow sticks or using small battery-operated string lights (make sure they don't get tangled as the wheel turns).

BUMPER CARS

Bumper cars zoom around on a flat rink, crashing into each other. They're easy to make from a few pieces of packaging.

WHAT YOU NEED

- Wide round plastic lids from food containers (black if possible)
- Plastic blister packs (plastic packaging from small items such as batteries, erasers, or dental floss)
- Thick cardboard, such as the side of a large cardboard box
- Card stock
- Toothpicks
- Small buttons or flat beads
- Scissors or a craft knife
- Superglue or a glue gun
- Paint and paintbrushes
- White glue
- A pencil and a marker
- A large cardboard box with a lid, such as a shoe box
- Four non-bendy straws
- Colored or metallic card stock (optional)

1 Turn your lid flat side facing up. If it's not black, paint it black using paint mixed with white glue to help it stick. Leave it to dry.

2 Draw and cut out a circle of thick cardboard, just slightly smaller than your lid. Cut out the plastic blister pack shape, leaving a small area of flat plastic around the edges.

3 Glue the flat part of the blister pack to the circle of cardboard. Draw an H shape on top of the blister pack and cut along the lines. Fold down the flaps inside the blister pack.

4 Cut out a strip of cardboard, the same width as the hole you made in the blister pack and four times as long. Fold it to make a seat. Glue it into the hole.

5 Paint the seat and upper part of the bumper car using paint mixed with white glue. Let it dry. Then glue them to the black lid bumper.

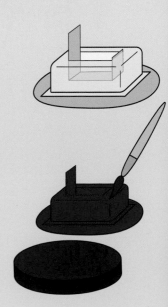

6 Cut a small steering wheel out of card stock. Color it black and glue it into the front of the seat. Make headlights from beads or buttons, and make a paper flag attached to a toothpick. Repeat steps 1 to 6 to make more bumper cars.

7 To make a rink, cut a bit more than 1 inch (3 cm) of the bottom off of the base of your large box. Tape four straws into the corners so they are standing.

8 Fit the box lid onto the tops of the straws. Tape it in place. Cut out a cardboard sign and tape or glue it to the front. Paint or decorate the rink. Cover the floor with brightly colored or metallic card stock.

BUMPER CARS

BUMPER CARS

THE SCIENCE PART!

On real bumper cars, the black bumper is made of rubber. When the bumper car gets hit, the rubber squashes, absorbing the shock, so the car itself doesn't get damaged. Regular cars have shock-absorbing bumpers, too.

TAKE IT FURTHER

To help your cars move around, try putting a handful of marbles under the lid part of each one.

CAROUSEL

The carousel is a famous, old-fashioned horse ride. Riders sit on brightly painted horses, which leap up and down to the sound of amusement park music.

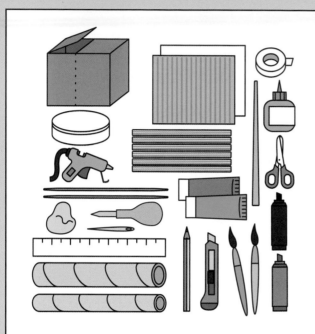

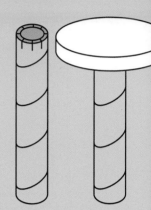

1 Cut about eight slits around the top of the wider cardboard tube, about 0.5 inches (1 cm) deep. Fold the tabs inward. Glue them to the inside of the round lid, right in the middle.

2 Turn the lid over and trace around it onto thick corrugated cardboard. Cut out the circle to make the base of the carousel. Stand the bottom of the wider tube in the middle of the circle and trace around it.

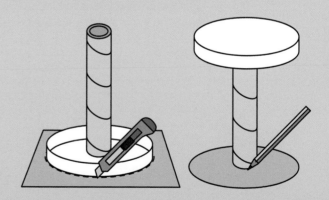

WHAT YOU NEED

- A round cardboard box lid, such as the lid from a round chocolate box
- Two cardboard tubes, one slightly narrower than the other
- Thick, strong cardboard, such as the side of a large cardboard box
- Twelve wooden skewers
- Six non-bendy straws
- A wooden chopstick or wooden stick
- White card stock
- Scissors or a craft knife
- A bradawl or a sewing needle
- A ruler and a pencil
- Paints and paintbrushes or markers
- White glue
- Superglue or a glue gun
- Clear tape
- Removable adhesive putty or soft modeling clay

MAKE THE HORSES MOVE!

This four-page project includes the option of making the horses move up and down, like they do on a real carousel. However, this is quite tricky, so you also have the option of just making them move in a circle, by only working up to step 13.

3 Cut the small circle out of the middle of the base. Fit the empty cardboard tube into the hole. Use glue or tape to put it together, if necessary. At this point, you can decorate the carousel with markers or paints mixed with white glue. Let it dry.

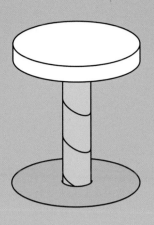

4 Mark six equally spaced points around the edge of the base. Make holes through them with the bradawl or sewing needle. Cut six pieces of straw, about 3 inches (8 cm) long.

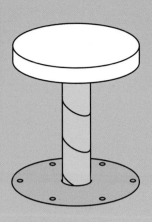

5 Push a wooden skewer through one of the holes in the base, then through a section of straw. Then push the top of the skewer up inside the lid, so that it lies flat against the inside edge.

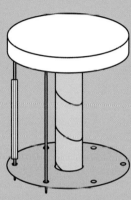

6 Tape the end of the skewer inside the lid. Repeat this for the other five skewers and straws.

7 With scissors, cut off the bottom of each skewer as neatly as possible, so that the base is flat and smooth underneath. Use a little glue or tape to keep the skewers in place, if necessary.

8 Measure the distance between the skewers. Copy a picture of a carousel horse onto smooth white card stock, making it slightly shorter than the distance you measured.

9 Cut out the horse and use it as a template to draw 11 more. Decorate them and cut them out. Glue two horses to each straw, one on each side, about two-thirds of the way up the straw.

TURN THE PAGE TO CONTINUE ...

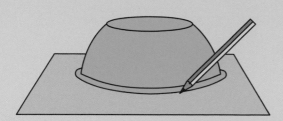

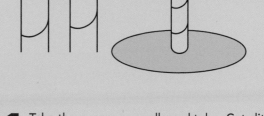

10 Make a circle larger than the carousel. Trace around a bowl or other object onto thick corrugated cardboard. Cut it out.

11 Take the narrower cardboard tube. Cut slits into one end of it, just like you did with the wider one. Fold the slits inward. Glue the tube to the middle of the large circle.

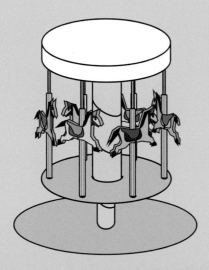

12 If needed, trim off the top of the narrower cardboard tube to make it shorter than the carousel. You can now fit the carousel onto it, so that it rests on the larger circle and can turn around.

13 Make a hole in the middle of the top of the carousel. Push the chopstick or other stick through it. You can use this to turn the carousel around.

TAKE IT FURTHER

Want to make the horses jump up and down too? Follow steps 14–19!

14 Cut a long strip of smooth card stock, about 2.5 inches (6 cm) wide and 10 inches (24 cm) long. Draw a line along its length, about 0.5 inches (1 cm) wide.

|← 10 inches (24 cm) →|

2.5 inches (6 cm)

15 Wrap the card stock strip around the carousel to make a circle a bit more than 0.5 inches (2 cm) wider than the base. Glue or tape it together and trim off any extra.

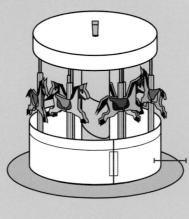

0.5 inches (2 cm)

16 Slip the circle off of the carousel. Cut slits along its edge, up to the line you drew. Fold the slits outwards. Mark six equal points around the circle. Draw lines to divide it into six sections.

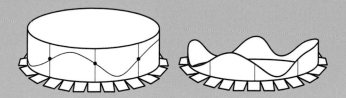

17 Draw a wavy line around the circle, going up and down with each section. Cut along the wavy line. Glue it to the base of the carousel, leaving a bit of space all the way round.

18 Cut six very small strips of smooth card stock. Glue them to the bottom ends of the straws to make loops. Each one should face the same way as the horse's head.

19 Take a new skewer and thread it through a loop. Put a pea-sized lump of adhesive putty or modeling clay on the end. Press it against the bottom of the central tube. Do the same for the five other horses. Trim off the ends, so that the skewers rest on the wavy cardboard circle.

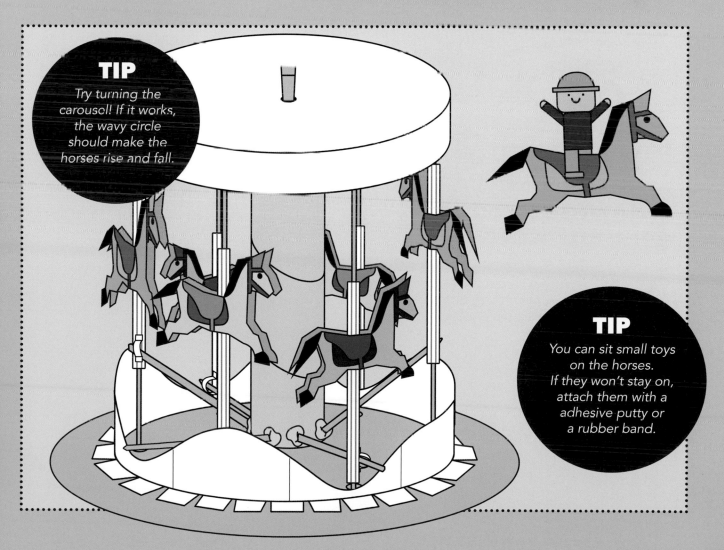

TIP

Try turning the carousel! If it works, the wavy circle should make the horses rise and fall.

TIP

You can sit small toys on the horses. If they won't stay on, attach them with a adhesive putty or a rubber band.

21

ROLLER COASTER

Are you ready for the roller coaster, the most frightening amusement park attraction of all? Some people love roller coasters and travel the world trying out all the most terrifying rides. Others won't go near them. But since you don't have to ride this coaster yourself, you can make it as exciting as you would like.

WHAT YOU NEED

- A large, shallow cardboard box, such as a pizza box
- Smaller cardboard boxes
- Lots of thick, smooth card stock
- Several long cardboard tubes, such as wrapping paper tubes
- Wooden skewers
- A small toy car
- Scissors or a craft knife
- Superglue or a glue gun
- Clear tape
- Masking tape
- A bradawl or a sewing needle
- A ruler and a pencil
- Paints and paintbrushes
- Markers

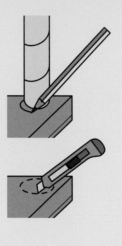

1 On the corner of your box, make a circle by tracing a cardboard tube. Carefully cut out the circle, slightly inside the line, so that the tube will fit tightly. Fit the tube into the hole.

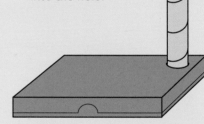

2 Do the same to the other corners of the box. This will give you enough towers to get started. You can add more later if you need to.

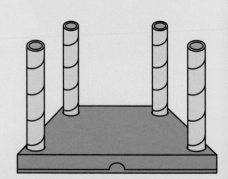

3 Before making the roller coaster track, sketch a design on paper. The track should join up in a loop, with a very high starting point so that the car rolls downhill.

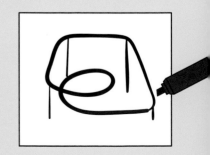

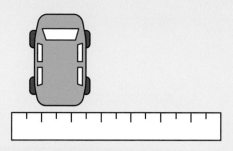

4 To make the track, first check the width of your toy car. The track should be around 1 inch (2.5 cm) wider than the car, so that it fits easily around the bends.

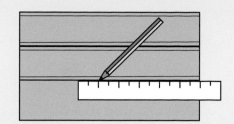

5 With a ruler and pencil, draw lengths of track onto smooth card stock, making them a width that will fit the car. To make the sides, add an extra 1 inch (2.5 cm) strip along each side of the track.

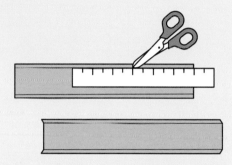

6 Cut out the pieces of track. Use a ruler and a scissor blade to press along the lines so that the sides can fold easily.

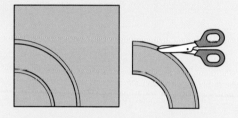

7 Make corners by drawing curved sections of track. Use a ruler to make sure you keep the track the same width all the way along and add sides. Cut out these pieces, too.

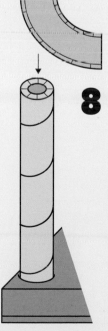

8 Build the roller coaster. Start at the top of the tallest tube. Cut 0.5-inch (1 cm) slits into the top of the tube, fold them inward, and glue a piece of track on top. You can use tape to strengthen it.

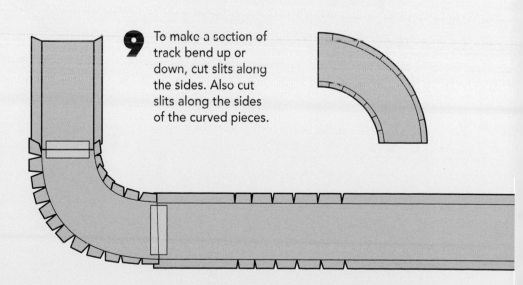

9 To make a section of track bend up or down, cut slits along the sides. Also cut slits along the sides of the curved pieces.

TURN THE PAGE TO CONTINUE ...

10 Add more sections as you go, taping them together to strengthen them. You can cut each piece of track to the length you need, or draw new sections to fit your design.

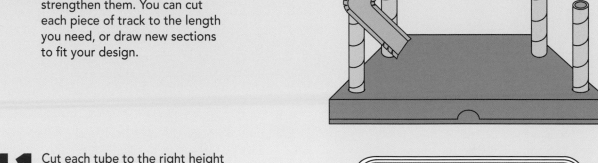

11 Cut each tube to the right height to support the track. Attach the track onto it. If you need to, add more tubes to the box or use wooden skewers as extra supports.

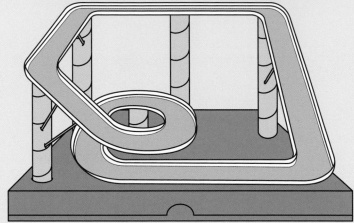

12 When the track is finished, fold the sides up along the edges. Fold lengths of masking tape (or clear tape) over the sides to hold them in place. You can now decorate the coaster with paint or markers.

13 To make your coaster car, cut a piece off a small cardboard box, such as a box of toothpaste. Make sure it is as narrow as the car. Put it on top of your toy car. Use tape to hold it in place, making sure the wheels can still turn.

14 Use smaller pieces of cardboard to divide the car into sections. If you like, decorate the coaster car with paints or markers.

15 Test the car on your roller coaster to see if it runs down the track. Fix any parts that are not working by smoothing them down with tape or adjusting the track.

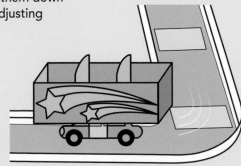

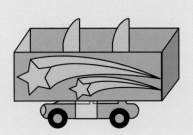

16 If there's space on your coaster, you can use another cardboard box to make a ticket office, with a doorway leading to the track and a sign on top.

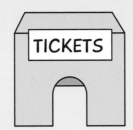

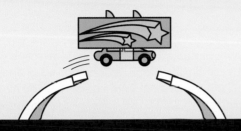

TIP

It can be tricky to make a roller coaster track that the car can run down. It needs to be smooth, with steep enough slopes for the car to build up speed, without going so fast that it flies off at the corners! Try making a simple track for your first attempt, to practice your skills. Then you can move on to more adventurous designs.

TAKE IT FURTHER

Once you're a master roller coaster builder, you can try adding more features:

- Can you build in a loop-the-loop?
- Can you build in a gap in the track that the car jumps across?
- Can you add more coaster cars and link them to make a train?

THE SCIENCE PART!

This roller coaster needs gravity to make it work. If your car builds up enough speed on a downhill section, it will have enough **momentum** to go up a small slope. But overall, the track must head downhill.

THE AMUSEMENT PARK

Now make an amusement park for all of your rides and stalls!

WHAT YOU NEED

- A very large piece of cardboard or several smaller pieces
- Thick smooth card stock
- A cereal box
- Straws or toothpicks
- Scissors or a craft knife
- Superglue or a glue gun
- Clear tape
- A bradawl or a sewing needle
- A pencil
- Paint and paintbrushes
- White glue
- Markers
- Lots of green fabric

You can get a really big piece of cardboard from the box of a large appliance, such as a washing machine. If you can't find one, tape several smaller pieces of cardboard together.

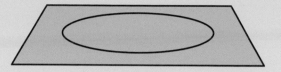

1 Trim your cardboard base to make it the shape you want. It can be any shape, as long as it's big enough to fit all the amusement park equipment you have made inside.

2 Most amusement parks are grassy, so paint the base green all over. You could also cover it with green cloth to make it look like grass instead.

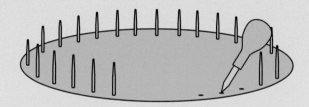

3 For the fence, make a row of holes along the edge of the cardboard using the bradawl or sewing needle. Stick a toothpick into each hole. You could also use pieces cut from straws. Make the holes bigger using the pencil, and fit a piece of straw into each hole. Remember to leave a gap in the fence for the entrance.

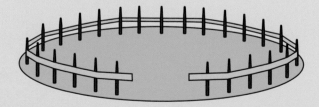

4 Cut strips of card stock about 0.5 inches (1 cm) wide. Glue them along the row of toothpicks or straws, just below the top. If you like, carefully paint the fence.

5 To make an entrance, draw an archway on the front of the cereal box. Cut out the doorway from both the front and the back of the box.

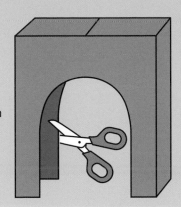

6 Cut a long strip of card stock (the length of the outline of the entrance). Place it in the gap between the front and back of the entrance, with an extra 0.5 inches (1 cm) along each side. Cut slits into the edge to make tabs. Carefully glue this strip along the inside edge of the doorway.

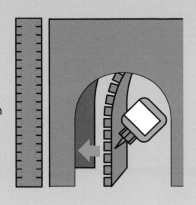

7 Cut out a sign shape, and glue or tape it to the top of the entrance. Decorate the entrance and sign using paint mixed with white glue. When it's dry, put it in the gap in the fence. (Remove part of the fence, if necessary.) Arrange your rides and stalls inside.

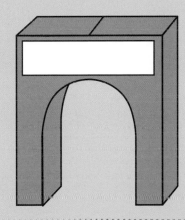

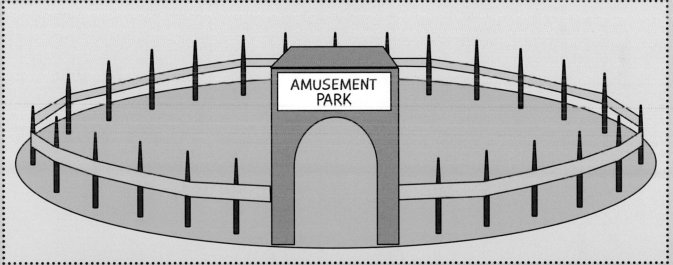

AMUSEMENT PARK

TAKE IT FURTHER

Carnivals have rides like amusement parks, and move from place to place. The people who work there sleep in trailers on the site. Can you make some workers' trailers?

AND HERE IS YOUR FINISHED AMUSEMENT PARK!

TICKETS

BUMPER CARS

AMUSEMENT PARK

GLOSSARY

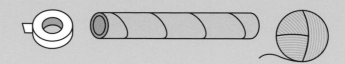

carousel An amusement park ride that spins around in a circle, usually with animals or vehicles to sit on or in

centrifugal force A pulling effect that makes objects move outward when they are whirled around in a circle

corkscrew roller coaster
A roller coaster with a section of track that twists around itself like a corkscrew

corrugated cardboard Thick cardboard with a layer of folded rows of paper inside it to make it stronger, often used to make cardboard boxes

Ferris wheels Giant rotating wheels with seats or cabins around the edge, named after its inventor George Ferris

glue gun An electric tool that heats up and applies strong glue

gravity Pulling force on objects. Earth's gravity pulls people and objects down to the ground.

helter-skelter A slide that travels in a downward spiral around the outside of a tower

momentum A force that makes a moving object keep on moving

spokes The rods that join the edge of a wheel to its center, giving the wheel its strength

template Something that is used as a basic shape or pattern to make lots of copies of something

FURTHER INFORMATION

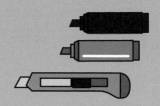

WHERE TO GET MATERIALS

Everyday items
You'll probably have some everyday items and craft materials at home already, such as foil, pens, tissues, string, paper, card stock, clear tape, glue, and scissors.

Recycling
Old packaging that's going to be thrown away or recycled is a great source of making materials, such as cardboard boxes, yogurt containers, paper towel tubes, magazines, old wrapping paper, and newspaper.

Grocery stores
Great for basic items you might not have at home, such as paper cups, cotton balls, a sewing kit, paper straws, toothpicks, and battery-powered string lights.

Outdoors
Collect items such as leaves, twigs, acorns, and shells for free!

Specialty stores
Craft stores, art stores, garden centers, and DIY stores could be useful for items such as a craft knife, a glue gun, white glue, modeling clay, fabric, sand, and pebbles.
If you don't have the store you need near you, ask an adult to help you search online.

Thrift stores
It's always a good idea to check thrift stores when you can, because they often have all kinds of household items and craft materials at very low prices.

BOOKS

Claybourne, Anna. *Gut-Wrenching gravity and other fatal forces*. Crabtree Publishing, 2013.

Cunningham, Kevin. *Roller Coasters: From Concept to Consumer*. Scholastic, 2013.

Mason, Paul. *How to Design the World's Best Roller Coaster: In 10 Simple Steps*. Wayland, 2019.

Spray, Sally. *Fairground Rides*. Capstone Press, 2018.

WEBSITES

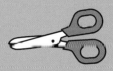

Amusement Park Physics
https://www.learner.org/interactives/parkphysics/
A website of interactive games and science facts about amusement park rides.

PBS Design Squad
https://pbskids.org/designsquad/
Visit this site for lots of great design and build challenges.

Parents.com Arts & Crafts
https://www.parents.com/fun/arts-crafts/?page=1
Check out maker projects, instructions, and videos.

INDEX